Pele

and the
Rivers of Fire

Adapted and Illustrated by

Michael Nordenstrom

BESS PRESS

3565 Harding Ave. Honolulu, Hawai'i 96816
808/ 734-7159   www.besspress.com

Library of Congress Cataloging-in-Publication Data

Nordenstrom, Michael.
Pele and the rivers of fire / adapted
and illustrated by Michael Nordenstrom.
p.   cm.
Includes illustrations and glossary.
ISBN 1-57306-079-8
ISBN 13 987-1-57306-079-0
1. Pele (Hawaiian deity) - Juvenile
literature. 2. Mythology, Hawaiian -
Juvenile literature. 3. Legends -
Hawaii - Juvenile literature. I. Title.
GR510.N67 2002   299.92-dc21

Printed in Korea

In respect for Pele
and
To my mother, Klea

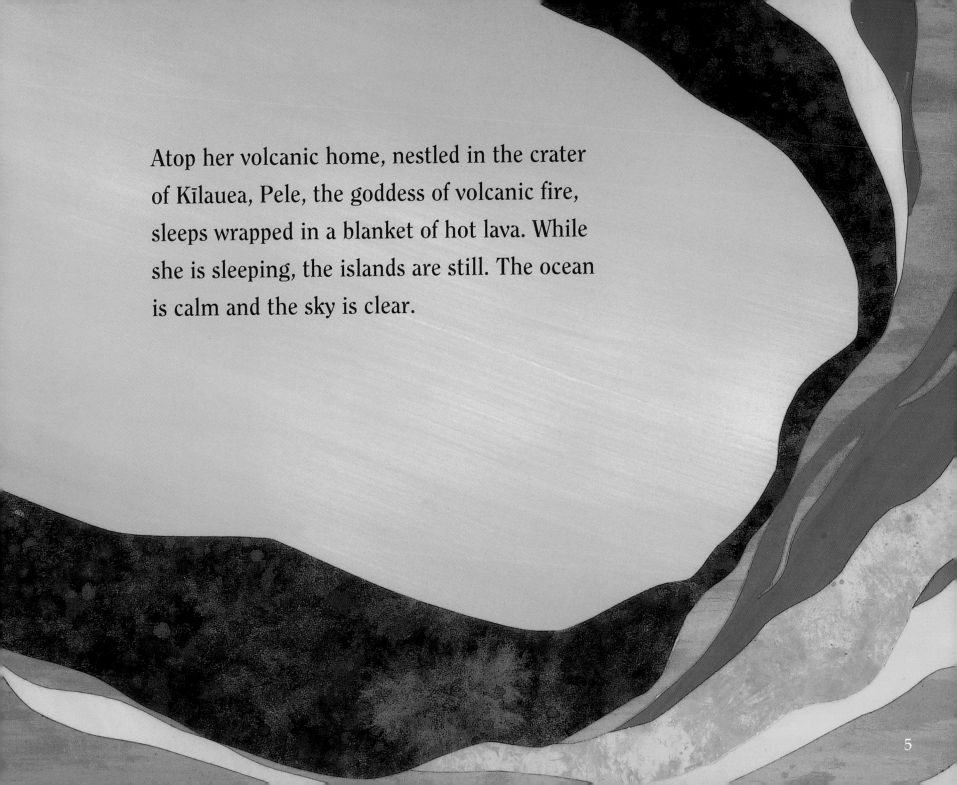

Atop her volcanic home, nestled in the crater of Kīlauea, Pele, the goddess of volcanic fire, sleeps wrapped in a blanket of hot lava. While she is sleeping, the islands are still. The ocean is calm and the sky is clear.

But Pele is a restless goddess, and when she wakes up, she causes quite a commotion. She rubs the sleep from her eyes and s-t-r-e-t-c-h-e-s her arms wide. This makes the volcano rattle and shake. And when she sits up, the land quakes.

She lets out a yawn that comes out as a

ROAR

and everyone knows
she's awake!

8

Then in a

BLAST

She bursts from her volcanic cauldron
in a fountain of fire and showers the slopes
with molten lava.

Pele watches as lava flows across mountainsides and
valleys. The fast-moving lava, called *pāhoehoe*,
forms rivers of fire that scorch the earth and leave
behind fields of blackened crust.

Slower moving lava, called ʻaʻā, creeps along and burns everything in its path. Trees, plants, and buildings are no match against the fiery river. Pele destroys all that is in her way.

Lava may flow until it reaches the ocean. When the hot lava collides with the cool Pacific water, a dense canopy of steam floats upward as the lava instantly hardens into stone.

Long ago, Pele journeyed across the sea
and brought her fire to the Hawaiian
Islands. She canoed from Kahiki to Kauaʻi,
guided by her shark brother, Kamohoaliʻi.

Pele left Kahiki because her sister, Nāmakaokahaʻi, continually put her fire out. But Nāmakaokahaʻi followed Pele and their brother to Kauaʻi, where she flooded Pele's new volcano with seawater. Furious, Pele moved on to Oʻahu, where she used her *pāoa* to dig an even deeper volcano. But still Nāmakaokahaʻi flooded it.

21

Pele moved from island to island. Then, on Maui, she and Nāmakaokahaʻi met in a violent battle. Pele was killed, and Nāmakaokahaʻi was certain Pele was finished.

But she **was wrong!**
Nāmakaokaha'i may have killed Pele's body, but she did
not kill her spirit. Soon Pele rekindled her flame and
became more powerful than ever.

With the help of her shark brother, Pele's spirit was guided to the island of Hawai'i. Here, Pele lives in a volcano so large and so deep her sister cannot flood it.

One day, Pele may make her home
in a new volcano, Lōʻihi,
now rising from the ocean floor.

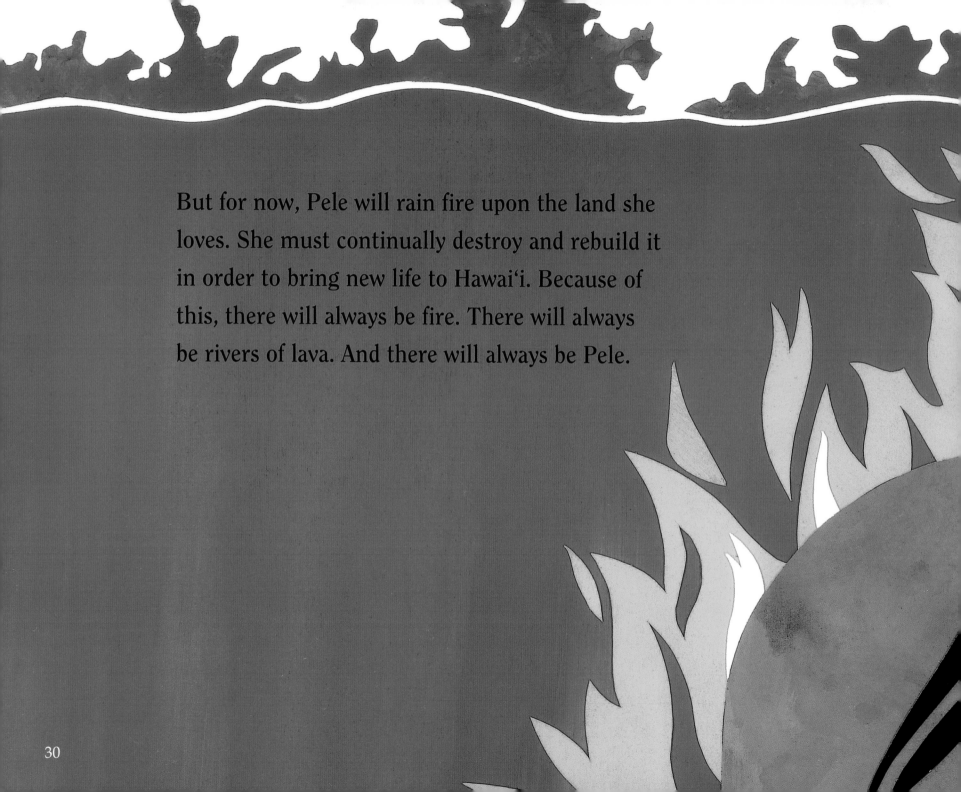

But for now, Pele will rain fire upon the land she loves. She must continually destroy and rebuild it in order to bring new life to Hawai'i. Because of this, there will always be fire. There will always be rivers of lava. And there will always be Pele.

Glossary

'a'ā (ah AH): lava that has a clinkery, or rough and jumbled, surface.

Kahiki (kah HEE kee): Tahiti, an island in French Polynesia, about 2,800 miles southeast of Hawai'i.

Kamohoali'i (kah moh hoh ah LEE ee): Pele's older brother, the shark god.

Kīlauea (KEE lau ay ah): a volcano on the island of Hawai'i.

Lō'ihi (LOH ee hee): a seamount forming off the southeast coast of the island of Hawai'i.

Nāmakaokaha'i (NAH mah kah oh kah hah ee): Pele's older sister, the sea goddess.

pāhoehoe (PAH hoy hoy): lava that has a smooth or ropy surface.

pāoa (PAH oh ah): Pele's digging stick.

Michael Nordenstrom is Associate Librarian and Volunteer Coordinator at the Salt Lake City Public Library. *Pele and the Rivers of Fire* blends his love for art and anthropology and embodies his belief in preserving legends. He uses collage, he says, because it "makes each picture its own work of art. The illustrations are a mix of acrylic and watercolor paints, which I apply to large sheets of paper. After drawing each picture, I cut and arrange the pieces as if they were a puzzle. I aim to weave a mixture of colors and patterns into each work." Visit his Web site to learn more: www.RiversofFire.com